I0210963

FINISHING LINE PRESS
www.finishinglinepress.com

motherlands

New Women's Voices Series, No. 190

poems by

Camille Hernandez

Finishing Line Press
Georgetown, Kentucky

motherlands

ISBN 979-8-89990-283-3 First Edition

ACKNOWLEDGMENTS

Variations of these poems first appeared in

So to Speak
Health Promotion Practice
Louisville Review,
Salt Hill Journal
Anaheim Poetry Review
Black Minds Magazine

Thank you for sharing my words with the world.

Publisher: Leah Huete de Maines
Editor: Christen Kincaid
Cover Art: Shann Daniels
Author Photo: Sandy Saravia
Cover Design: Elizabeth Maines McCleavy

Order online: www.finishinglinepress.com
also available on amazon.com

Author inquiries and mail orders:
Finishing Line Press
PO Box 1626
Georgetown, Kentucky 40324
USA

Contents

for my mother and the ones who mothered me

overwhelm, a colonial swarm

That summer was the time of flies. Dawning into our
neighborhoods, touching every orifice of our sense of self.

Their squirming children arose in hoards, outgrowing our
capacity to resist. Our children swapped their toy swords for

fly swatters, running through suburbia with newly minted
slaying skills protecting what was once ours.

What now belongs to them. Flies do not borrow.

We took paradise from a fig tree. A ripe fruit word *ferdous*
pops out of your lips, riding the breath until your teeth unleash

a burst birthing the slithering snake from its bloom.
Ferdous means garden, not like an orchard

but like the labyrinth of laundry hung in our yards.
Every rope a vine, every baby gown a sprouted leaf.

My cousin called just as I was grabbing mail.
She witnessed my haunting in 4K. I cradled hers. "It's terrible here,

it's hell." She complained from a collapsing ocean where Lahaina
burned, families unable to find each other, water rerouted to resorts,

the tourism industry protecting the eroding pockets of vacationers.
Their plight set mold on my inconvenience ; this birthplace of crisis.

dinnertime

There are two types of dinners: one with rice and one without.
Dinners are riceless when the cheeks are too fat and skin

jiggles like a polygraph from our bone. Truth is, men like it
when we look gaunt. It reminds them of the glory days when a

good American soldier rescued skinny starving woman from the
burning grass huts his battle buddies set aflame. Fantasies are

decoration only, but no one tells them this. Delusions are safe.
We affix our eyes and tell our comrades that he's a fine piece

of work. He wants to hear that he's an Adonis. He wants you to
choke on it a little, it'll make him feel like a man. I once choked

on a piece of bread and accidentally made eye contact with a
good American church boy. I became a voracious prayer. God

protect me from this carnivore. He's so hungry. I've abolished
my appetites but hunger screams in different ways. Like how

aid trucks on Harun al-Rashid Street meet two kinds of hunger:
people needing aid and people needing more war stories to tell

their loved ones back home. The most expensive bag of flour
costs
one hundred and twelve Palestinians. The souls flow like wine as

Shrapnel scents the air. I don't eat dinner tonight. I rinse rice
Three times to rid the dust and starch.

look what I can do

he climbs a pillared playground as mothers
milk slips from his toddling smile. we play

peek-a-boo between each gap. in a near distance
his mama speaks slow measures of a second

language: “your honor, the legal aid said we can’t
apply for asylum.” the judge presses her lips to this

hanging silence of a courtroom. the child dangles
from the partition   his is the only pride here

daisy chain

springtime
we
harvested
worrisome
blues
threading
them
together
into
halos
of
hope
crowning
us
gloriously

the chair
growing
known
flowers
cried
needles
from
our
powerlessness
electrocuting
somebody's
child
was
executed
today

zip-zaps
information
from
generating
folly
to
us
turning
what
names
staunch
witness
in
affliction
unhindered

Pellie, Pele, and me

Daughters who seldom   listen, know these
islands we become are   a second-generation
hardness reaching back   across an ocean our
mamas didn't want to   leave. My mama was
named after the sea   by a landlocked woman.
My mama changed   her name after she crossed
herself. (Or so the   immigration papers say.)
When she landed   on the soil she renamed
herself an American   volcano (because women
must be made of ash   and lava to survive.)
Sometimes I check   the tides for the regrets
she drowned but   when mama extends her
anxieties, I return to   the cavity in her chest, and
when Mama chooses   silence, my archipelago
branches toward what   mythology gets left behind
with abandoned names

aunty culture, part 1

—and it was when hail fell on our aunties house that I was vulnerable enough to tell who I could of the moment I received no grace. In your office I was lying back down, defenseless as the babies blessed my perineal tears, recalling the ancestral aunties who are withheld from our knowledge of history. I imagined me holding each woman down in a blessed way as they grinded their teeth until the wicks of flesh are all the evidence of their will to live as blasphemed women. I was saying prayers to them and envisioning how growing our bonds of our ache would incite the fruit of our rage. I used all our aunties names: Anarcha, Betsy, and Lucy. I saw how their screams bore thread stitching up every exam table and how their tenderness towards each other made them mothers in strife. What can I know of medicine besides it horrors? We hold up our ankles and stifle each scream as we wait for everyone who knows of more medical terminology than us to document the ways our wombs wither now and at each moment we remember that these lifesaving procedures were built on torture. As the ice pummeled my auntie's house I watched her form the word resistance in her wrinkled woe. "Come, baby," she said, "I'll repay you for sharing that memory with me. It seems the ancestors haven't let of go your hand. There are many debts we are called to remember."

hail our aunties who received
no grace. your perineal tears,
are with me blessed
are the blasphemed women.
and growing are the fruit of our rage. all
our aunties mothers of medicine
scream for everyone
now and at each moment our resistance
i repay y your debts

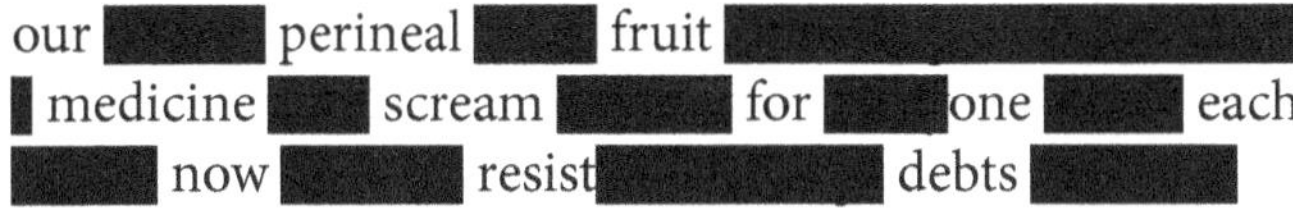

our perineal fruit
medicine scream for one each
now resist debts

[hoop] [gloss] [womb] [loss]

they say the wider the [ ] the bigger the ho-
liness found in forgotten passed down traditions.
there is no one to braid the hair-map. few who
speak of this [ ], and the atrocities of having it
or having no one to touch Black girl [ ]. magical
living is tiring. speak devotion into the [ ]. how
else do you expect the spells to take root?
by the hole in her [ ]? when a Black girl uncovers
her [ ] for the first time she become goddess-
queen, recoverer of memory. watch the [ ]. see
how it shines. unwrap the [ ] let it straighten her
posture, elongate the neck, and burry it deep
within a cloud of witnesses secured by [ ] they're
watching the way she inherits their [ ], how she
alchemizes it into an unbound effort to survive.

anthems

my son counts to
two-hundred
in many languages
marking calendars, making songs
with his newly gained
knowledge held, but
I press him for more
high expectations, these
urges to see numbers fluidly
rivers to seas
way we count insatiable
memories of witnessing terror
turn lands and people into a tar—

my country 'tis
tis wee sweet
land of liberty
of thee I sing
land where my
fathers died
land of the
pilgrim's pride
from
every
mountainside
let freedom
ring

homelands duplex

I wake him early and wash his wounds
he does not want to see the ghost limb crusting

he does not watch how the ghost is crusting
I measure the water's heat to match my calm

I pray that water's heat will match my calm
each May through October I hear of monsoons

may I hear the monsoons of October
be whispers with love from Aman Sinaya

I tried to whisper amen with love
held my breath to forget a cast off smell

my cast off breath can forget to tell
a motherland of no memories I reach

I reach for memories of a motherland
I wake early to wash all our wounds

a humidity called pre-grief

how will
I remain when
your country is cold and
my only limb to it is lost?
mama, I buried the
sun in soil to
heed us.

grandmama lost her leg but actually

it was amputated. she would tell her caretakers of how it itched or needed a stretch. She would lie in bed complaining about pain of unremembered absence. grandmama never cried. just talked as I walked knobby kneed ash speckled legs to the hallway. my hope a struck down tree decayed me into a stump. at her doorway my roots hallowed. the leg was lost in a corkscrew forest cultivating time and tragedy. years of diabetes stress sugar pills and living for scraps off the table and being the daughter of enslaved peoples and high yellow skin with no one to trust and more mouths to feed than liturgies to pray and pesticides in Mississippi delta water and hypertension and high blood pressure existing in great grandmother's chest long before grandmama's heart beat. grandmama wasn't doomed to depart from her leg, the cruelty of this world doomed her to miss herself. this is how I learned of ubuntu. somewhere in time our spirits were amputated and up until this very moment I could only talk about the itch that was the longing to be connected back to you

motherlands

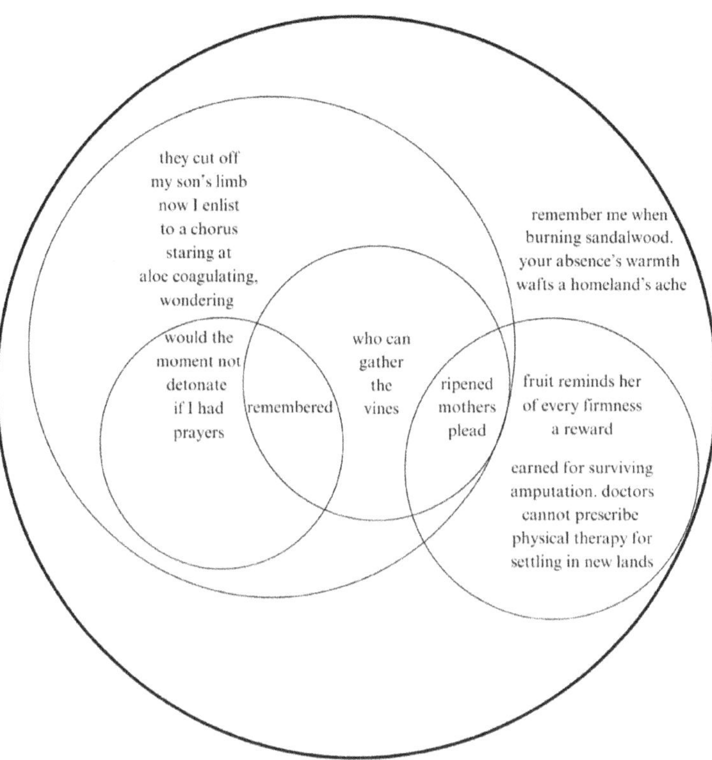

aunty culture, part 2

for Ray Anne, after Jacqueline Jones Lamon

my miracles aren't made of water and wine
we formed them in tears whispering liturgies
our hands. our words. our fears. our embrace.

against a whetted reaper starving for prayers
each lash line exalted a poorly secured border
my miracles aren't made of water and wine

mothers grow harmonies of unarchived breaths
who shudder and collapse inside weeping bones
our hands. our words. our fears. our embrace.

all parts desperate and exposed with no parasol
to shield us from this burning grief of living
my miracles aren't made of water and wine

children play as we web the salt within us
we cast a net hauling in their wriggling beliefs
our hands. our words. our fears. our embrace.

we built a sanctuary of abnormal cells and stone
we women who chart maps with our heartache
my miracles aren't made of water and wine
our hands. our words. our fears. our embrace.

Al Shifa Hospital Cento

mother, I miss you
what god has written for us will not despair
its title is in tears and pain
of a besieged person looking for medication
will only leave with god's permission
in worshipping you

mother
God
relief is near
wipe away the tears that fall onto my cheek
inside the heart of freedom

is tears and pain
god willing

the pain inside me will fall and land
on a mountain
god willing
relief is the well-known story
that god's permission
would collapse

mercy   mercy   mercy

tricksternometry

1+i
There is Coyote in the shape of me
holding a clay pot, collecting rain water
I wish it had a hole. There is acid in the
rain, or so the non-locals say. The pot
will not hold, it will melt soon.

1-i
Coyote takes the full pot to Badgers home.
"What will I do with a pot of drowning
water?" She asks her husband. "I do
not know," I reply. Coyote and Badger hold
hands and tip over the rainwater.

±(1+i)
Every droplet is a memory.

√I
I want to dissolve the rain into salt. May
it protect the ghosts in my wounds.

0 + 1i
Coyote wants to crack the cistern. "It's less
damage," we say.

0.707 + 0.707i
We are no longer coyote shaped. I slither to
the shards wanting to relive how to collect
rainwater. But there's other places to drown.

shy plant

time is a curse of mosquitos laying eggs and gossip,
there you'll find a girl with leaves and limbs tangling
from delicate pores to fetal position and mama's prayers

it happened before her blossoming

dreams tangled into the squash vines as spikes protect
innocence left unnamed. rosemary and lavender waft
to invite little hands crafting dents into her essence.

it happened before her blood

a girl so diligent and pure she's made of one thousand
paper mâché sampaguita sorrows protected by a prayer
from a howling tsunami and the Remington melodies

it happened before her thighs swallowed a pistol

one plant in the garden hears the plead—"*God, please
keep my child safe*"—once a quiet girl, now she's dew
collecting grieving centuries ignited from a slain mother.

folded sonnet for overdue phone calls

humm goes the fading battery. warning. warning. warning.
quickening the plot and introducing tenacity
to what hangs in the air. i know how to receive you
now the distance from our past matches the biomes between us.
i am a serial killer: my phone will die again,
and i will reap every placid reward of your voice fading.
dementia set our choreography. do you get scared
of forgetting? of how we're forgotten? i set routines
in photos: remember my kids? they're in the __ grade now, see?
rituals making up for sins i can't own. I poem
my regrets. i fold the verses because the miles won't crumple.
there's uncried fables i need you to heal. are we victims
or do we bumble ourselves out of this ghostliness? forgive
me, in ignoring you i cosigned our loneliness.

golden hour

"Miss Zora Neale Hurston," Aaron Douglas, 1926

simple feasts

tickle the nose

blue painted tunes

shading

all the browns

we are

doing

our best

genius is

lovemaking

kinda love too boring

for short attention

spans

a missing country

in the way cheeks slant

when you've caught

a

good

word

like

pennies

under the cushion

the tower of babel is a queer coded love story

"I learned how to be trans in
the Catholic Church"
Geena Rocero

when a curiosity falls from the sky / and stones
topple off a prayer shaft nicknamed / tower
you wipe your lips / & remember how
phallic things were made to pierce heaven
all theology / is architectural wet dreaming   listen
a shield stops gyrating harmonies / is
                                                    g _ d's hormones
spilling cocaine bumps of / false devotion /   found
faith turned fallacy as fists walloped
in the name of j _ _ _ us / we become the   foreign objects
chanting catechisms like torn perineal
 muscles / because we miss / it /   the genderless dark
survival touches the flesh / between
e t e r n i t y ' s fingers / keep your head up /   those
fists will fall / from the sky / shattering   spines
like xylophones out of order / & heavy / souls   pressed
to the ground will find / no hell under our feet
wiser now / as remaining rubble / naïvely held   against
every star reaching for a single taste of /   us

the poet considers her canvas

had it not been for laundry lounging
seductively, one could notice a sunset
winking those solar eyelashes amidst
rhapsodies of colors ; she beckons me

from her chaise freshly bathed and un-
touched by aging; it's the way she needs
me to caress crease fluff fold every

stiffness from her form doing her very
best to starve my senses, but I say yes

because my hands are soft and generous

second generation labyrinth

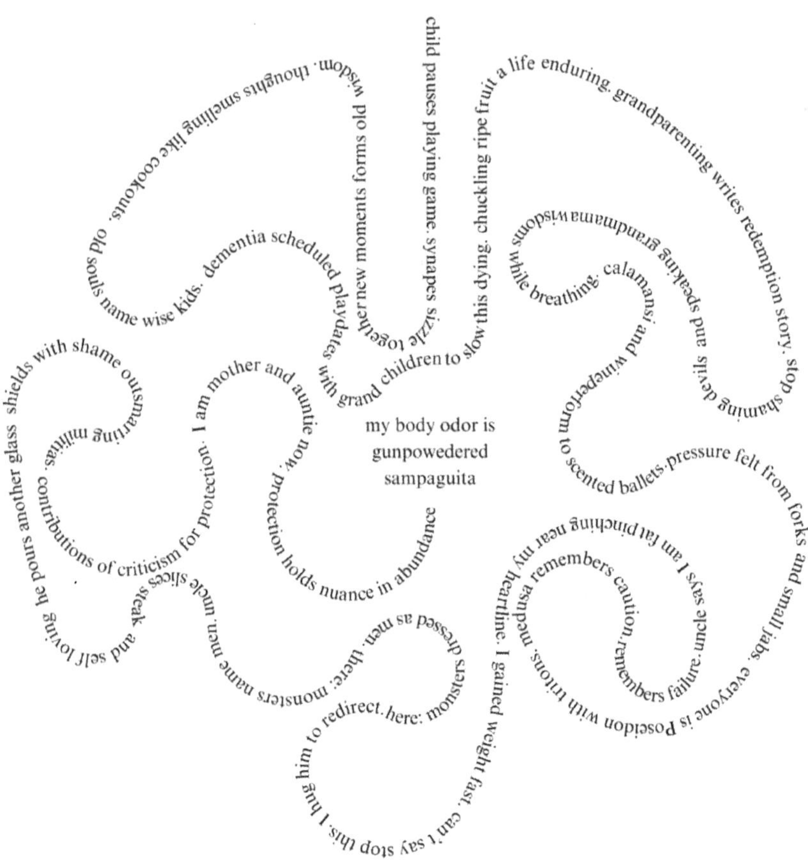

Delores Huerta at the PTA meeting

life filled with
bellies

WE FEED YOU

hands wrinkled with
laughter

SI SE PUEDE

bakers dozen of
reasons

COME JOIN US

mothers and children passing
markers

SUPPORT FARMWORKERS

every crackling thundered
hand

BOYCOTT

offering plates of fruit-
stained cardboard

HUELGA

American hieroglyphs on
overused sheets

COME JOIN US

ode to the tsimosa I am becoming

my favorite thing about girl power is
there's no power in the world that could
survive vibrations made from those lips who
dragged a cigarette and chose not to proclaim
all your dirty laundry to the rest of this barrio.
her skin is soil. her hair: smoke. a goddess of
roots and clouds. ready to burry secrets and
enchant every ear to her wind. her voice
tastes like thunder, her advice is the texture
of sage. there is truth in every single one of
her lies. her lies are smiling at how you listen
to her stories. each wrinkle is evidence of her
love. she loves this neighborhood the way a trick-
ster loves the consequence. faithfully returning
us to the glory of story, contracting
this community's swollen heartbeat.

aunty culture, part 3

1.
we write memoirs in food scraps left behind
"Aunty, can you open the crab for me?" she asks
digging my thumb into its armor I free vulnerabilities
forming them into pyramids, each an artifact or mystery

2.
there are no forks on the table
a machete rests near the doorway
tired from a long day of nursing

3.
the word is *magkamay*, to eat with bare hands
I cannot loose fingertips of conquest from
my muscle buttons, silence is a blanket tucking
our lingering curiosities goodnight

4.
"making hamay" accepts all the ways we crack

5.
in another country, my uncle stirs ice cold grits
as aunty inhales the ways I play with her twang in
the gaps between my fingers. Their love teaches me
to wield inheritances of bladed wisdoms

6.
there is no word for breathing between generations.
Come mourning light, I'll tie my nightgown
at my knees to fertilize the sky
and gaze at the soil

7.
I am insecure about my body being
two countries tall and an ocean wide
my hipbones hold tallies of generations

surviving. My salambao is bellybutton
tall, brown as a promise. I cast
nets into an unmarked constellation
of claws protecting each other

Camille Hernandez is the Poet Laureate for the City of Anaheim. Her writing explores the fluidity of intimacy through devotion, dogma, and tenderness. Her previous work has appeared in *Braving the Body, Health Promotion Practice, Louisville Review*, and *So to Speak*. Her debut memoir, *The Hero and the Whore*, debuted as the #1 new release on Amazon's Sociology of Abuse category. Camille has been named a Finishing Line Press' New Women Voices Chapbook finalist and a semifinalist for TulipTree Publisher's 2025 Wild Woman storytelling competition. She's a fellow with The Watering Hole.

As the literary ambassador to a globally influential city, Camille represents the ways love shows up amid violence. Her captivating words and reflective worldview have been enjoyed internationally through her bestselling books and poetry performances. Camille was born and raised in Orange County, CA by immigrants and civil rights organizers. She attended UC Santa Cruz where she studied the politics of culture and received her MA in Educational Leadership. Her poetry highlights the surprising ways love and tenderness manifest in our deepest connections and celebrates hope as part of our intergenerational lineage.

When she's not writing, Camille enjoys collecting chunky jewelry and going camping with her family.

www.ingramcontent.com/pod-product-compliance
Lightning Source LLC
Chambersburg PA
CBHW022101080426
42734CB00009B/1440